D0273692

Owls

Laura Marsh

NATIONAL
GEOGRAPHIC

Washington, D.C.

For my wise sisters-in-law: Betsy, Carrie, and Julie
— L.F.M.

The publisher and author gratefully acknowledge the expert review
of this book by Paul T. Zeph, National Audubon Society

Browse the complete Collins catalogue at
www.collins.co.uk

ISBN: 978-0-00-826661-5
US Edition ISBN: 978-1-4263-1743-9

Book design by YAY! Design

Cover, Scott Linstead/Foto Natura/Minden Pictures; 1, George F. Mobley/National Geographic Creative; 4–5, Steve Bloom Images/
Alamy; 6, PeterVrabel/Shutterstock; 7 (UPLE), Juniors Bildarchiv GmbH/Alamy; 7 (UPRT), Igor Kovalenko/Shutterstock; 7 (LOLE), jtairat/
Shutterstock; 7 (LORT), Stephen Mcsweeny/Shutterstock; 8, Alaska Stock/Alamy; 9, Tom Vezo/Minden Pictures; 10–11, Michael Nichols/
National Geographic Creative; 12, blickwinkel/Alamy; 13, Valerio Pardi/Shutterstock; 14, Paul Mcmullen/Flickr/Getty Images; 15, Melinda
Fawver/Shutterstock; 16–17, Tom Vezo/Minden Pictures; 18, Robbie George/National Geographic Creative; 19, Roberta Olenick/Getty
Images; 20 (UP), Erwin Van Laar/Foto Natura/Minden Pictures; 20 (LO), Joe McDonald/Visuals Unlimited/Getty Images; 21 (UP), Thomas
Dressler/Gallo Images/Getty Images; 21 (LO), Christina Bollen/Oxford Scientific RM/Getty Images; 22–23 (Background), Carsten Reising-
er/Shutterstock; 22 (UP), Tadashi Shimada/Nature Production/Minden Pictures; 22 (CTR), Guy Edwardes/Photographer's Choice/Getty
Images; 22 (LO), Kennan Ward/Corbis; 23 (UP), Michael Cummings/Flickr RF/Getty Images; 23 (UPRT), Thomas Kitchin & Victoria Hurst/
First Light/Getty Images; 23 (CTR), Joel Sartore/National Geographic Creative; 23 (LO), Dave King/Dorling Kindersley/Getty Images; 24,
Jane Burton/Getty Images; 25, Michio Hoshino/Minden Pictures; 26, Jane Burton/naturepl.com; 27, Art Wolfe/Iconica/Getty Images; 28,
Gerard Lacz/FLPA/Minden Pictures; 30 (LE), Peter Reynolds/Frank Lane Picture Agency/Corbis; 30 (RT), Panu Ruangjan/Shutterstock; 31
(UPLE), Edwin Giesbers/naturepl.com; 31 (UPRT), Steve Maslowski/Visuals Unlimited/Getty Images; 31 (LOLE), Michael Duva/Stone Sub/
Getty Images; 31 (LORT), Emil von Maltitz/Gallo Images/Getty Images; 32 (UPLE), Christina Bollen/Oxford Scientific RM/Getty Images; 32
(UPRT), Art Wolfe/Iconica/Getty Images; 32 (LOLE), Wayne Lynch/All Canada Photos/Corbis; 32 (LORT), Guy Edwardes/Photographer's
Choice/Getty Images; top border of pages, vareennik/Shutterstock; vocabulary boxes, valeriya_sh/Shutterstock

Printed and bound in China by RR Donnelley APS

MIX
Paper from
responsible sources

FSC
www.fsc.org

FSC™ C007454

Table of Contents

Who Are You?

What hoots in the night
and flies through the air?

snowy owl

What has feathers and big eyes,
but does not have hair?

You may never see one,
but you'll know if you do.

Did you guess? Yes?
It's an owl, that's who!

Many Owls

There are more than 155 kinds of owls. Owls can be big or small. Their faces can be round or shaped like a heart.

barn owl

eagle owl

Eastern screech owl

Owls come in lots of colours and patterns.

Oriental bay owl

great grey owl

Owls Everywhere

barred owl

great horned owl

Owls live in cold places and hot places. They live in rain forests and deserts. Owls also live in the mountains and near the ocean.

Hotshot Hunters

Owls are great fliers. They are also great hunters. Most owls hunt at night. Their bodies are made for hunting.

EARS: Great ears help owls hear animals they want to eat. An owl can hear a mouse on the ground 23 metres away.

WINGS: Strong wings move quickly and quietly.

northern spotted owl

EYES: Owls see better at night than any other bird. They can spot their food quickly in the dark.

BEAK: A sharp, curved beak tears meat into bits.

FEET: Powerful feet pounce on food.

TALONS: They grab and carry food.

Bird Box

TALONS: Sharp claws on birds that hunt and eat meat

Owls watch their prey carefully. But they can't move their eyes. They turn their heads to follow their prey.

little owl

Bird Box

PREY: An animal that is eaten by another animal

short-eared owl

Owl heads turn much further than
human heads do. Owls can see
behind them. They can even twist
their heads almost upside down!

short-eared owl

Owls are quiet fliers. They can
sneak up on their prey.

An owl has special feathers on its wings. The feathers have extra-soft edges. They make the wings quiet. Prey cannot hear the owl flying toward it.

Dinnertime!

Western screech owl

Many owls eat small animals like mice. Some owls eat insects, snakes, or fish. Other owls even eat small birds and bigger animals, too.

Owls do not chew their food.
They don't have teeth.
Owls tear food with their
sharp beaks. Or they eat their
prey whole.

Owl Homes

young great horned owls

Owls travel to different areas to hunt. So they don't call one place home. They often just pick a tree to rest in.

But young owls stay in or near a nest. They stay until they learn to fly. Owl nests may be in trees or on the ground.

young burrowing owls

Hide and Seek

These owls are hiding.
Can you find them?

They look like the land
and trees around them.
This is called camouflage.
It helps the owls stay safe
from enemies.

Bird Box

CAMOUFLAGE: An animal's
natural colour or shape
that blends in with what
is around it

short-eared owl

African scops owl

snowy owl

little owl

21

7 Cool Owl Facts

1

Owls have feathers all over their bodies. They even have feathers on their legs.

2

The Eurasian eagle owl has a very large wingspan. Its wings stretch about as long as your sofa!

3

The elf owl is the smallest owl. It is about as tall as a mobile phone.

4 Great grey owls can hear a mouse moving under deep snow. Their talons grab the mouse through the snow.

5 Great horned owls are not picky eaters. They are the only animals that often eat skunks.

ear

6 Owls don't have ears that stick out like ours do. Their ears are just holes on the sides of their heads.

7 Owls have two toes in the front and one in back. A fourth toe can move either way to help grab things.

Bird Box

WINGSPAN: The length from the tip of one wing to the tip of the other wing

A Nest of Babies

A mother owl lays about two to six eggs at one time. She sits on the eggs until they hatch.

Owls that have just hatched have soft, fluffy feathers. Young owls are called owlets.

Q What did the owl parents say to the baby owl that asked to stay up late?

A Sorry, you are not owld enough!

snowy owl owlets

tawny owl owlet

Every day the owlets grow bigger.
They grow new feathers, too.

The father owl often brings food to the family. The owlets learn to fly and hunt as they get older.

great owls

Who Hoots?

Cape Eagle owl

Try making a hooting call out of your window at night. Then listen carefully. An owl just might return your call!

But not all owls hoot. Different owls have different calls. Some owls screech. Others hiss, whistle, or even bark. What can you hear?

What in the World?

These pictures show close-up views of owls. Use the hints below to work out what's in the pictures. Answers are on page 31.

HINT: They can carry dinner.

HINT: These are all over an owl's body.

WORD BANK

feathers   beak   eyes   owlet   talons   wings

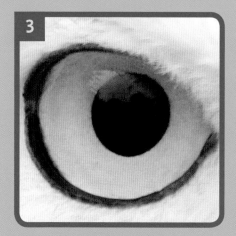

HINT: They work well, even in the dark.

HINT: A young owl is called this.

HINT: Owls need these to fly.

HINT: An owl uses this instead of teeth.

Answers: 1. talons, 2. feathers, 3. eyes, 4. owlet, 5. wings, 6. beak

CAMOUFLAGE: An animal's natural colour or shape that blends in with what is around it

PREY: An animal that is eaten by another animal

TALONS: Sharp claws on birds that hunt and eat meat

WINGSPAN: The length from the tip of one wing to the tip of the other wing